BOBBIE
THE WONDER DOG

A True Story

Written *by* TRICIA BROWN

Illustrated *by* CARY PORTER

WEST
MARGIN
PRESS

Bobbie was going on vacation!

Just as his favorite man finished securing the luggage, the mixed-breed collie jumped up in one easy leap. This would be his riding place.

"Let's go!" Bobbie seemed to say, wagging his stumpy tail.

On that hot summer day in 1923, he didn't know that he was leaving on the trip of a lifetime. Bobbie couldn't know that by next year, he—just a regular farm dog from Silverton, Oregon—would be famous.

Today all he cared about was a ride with his people.

BRAZIER

Bobbie's people were Frank and Elizabeth Brazier and their daughters, Leona and Nova. Two years earlier, Frank had decided their farm needed a farm dog. He went to the neighbor's to inspect a new litter.

There, in the pile of six-week-old fluffballs, one yipped for Frank's attention. Something about the pup was different . . .

"How 'bout that? He's got a bobbed tail!" Frank said, picking up the puppy. "I'll take him."

And that's how Bobbie got a name *and* a home.

On the farm, Bobbie was a spunky puppy and a natural
"heeler," nipping at the heels of cows, cats, and even people,
to make them go where he wanted. But one time a stubborn horse
kicked back at Bobbie. Even with a bad cut above one eye, little
Bobbie pestered that horse into the corral.

Just months later, Bobbie had another close call when his leg
was run over by a tractor.

"That'll leave another scar," Frank said, as he gently bandaged the wound.

As soon as he could walk again, Bobbie eagerly went back to work.

There was no stopping Bobbie.

When the Braziers decided to quit farming to run a restaurant in town, they didn't know what to do about Bobbie.

"A herding dog needs to be on a farm," Frank said. But inside he was thinking, *How can I sell my best friend*?

"We have to do what's best for Bobbie," Elizabeth said. They decided it was best to leave him on the farm with the new owners, where he could run free and continue herding. Saddened, the family gave Bobbie extra pets, snacks, and belly rubs.

When they left Bobbie behind, he was sad, too.

Days later, Bobbie ambled into their restaurant, as if to say, "Hey, didn't you forget somebody?" He had walked for miles, yet he knew right where to go.

"Aw, Bobbie, you can't be in here," Frank said as he stroked the dog's head. "People don't want fur in their food." He took the young dog back to the farm.

But a few days later, Bobbie was back.

"We need to talk," Elizabeth said to Frank. That evening, the country people and the town people reached an agreement: on weekdays, Bobbie would work on the farm; on weekends, he'd stay in town.

Bobbie agreed, too.

The idea worked for a while, but by summer, Frank and Elizabeth missed Bobbie terribly. So they bought him back from the farmer . . . for three times more than they'd sold him for.

When August rolled around, they planned a trip back to their old hometown. With Bobbie, of course.

The trip from Silverton, Oregon, to Wolcott, Indiana, was 2,551 miles—days and days of driving on unpaved "auto trails." Bobbie was in dog heaven.

From his perch, he scanned the horizon like a king inspecting his domain.

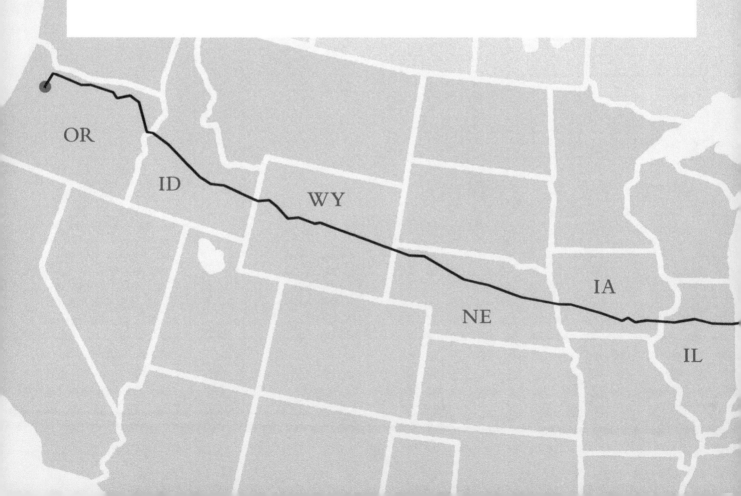

In 1923, there were no highways. The dirt roads were dusty, narrow, and bumpy, and cars moved a lot slower. Often the Braziers' car was the only one around.

Through the long days, Bobbie entertained himself. If he spotted a rabbit, he launched off the car and raced after it. Sometimes an hour would pass before he returned to the road. As Bobbie neared, Frank slowed a bit, so he could hop aboard.

"Bobbie sure makes a long trip more fun, doesn't he?" Frank said. Elizabeth smiled and nodded.

The Braziers never worried. No matter how far away their dog ran, no matter how tired he got, he always found his way back. There was no stopping Bobbie.

Through the Rocky Mountain passes . . .

. . . and across the Great Plains,

the Braziers drove east, sending up dust clouds through

Idaho . . .

   Wyoming . . .

                           Nebraska . . .
         Iowa . . .

                  Illinois . . .

At last, Elizabeth read a border sign:

"INDIANA! We're almost there!"

At last, the dusty car pulled up to a house full of relatives. Bobbie wiggled and licked as his people hugged and shook hands. Then Frank checked his watch. "I'm going to gas up the car now, while I can," he said. "Back soon. Let's go, Bobbie!"

At the filling station, Bobbie slipped off to look around. Suddenly, Frank saw him racing around a corner, chased by a pack of snarling dogs. Frank shook his head. *Bobbie knows his way out of trouble*, he thought. *He won't be long.*

The tank was filled, the bill was paid, but Frank was still waiting. He tooted his car horn. That usually worked. He cupped his hands and called, "Let's go, Bobbie!"

Nothing.

He's probably gone back to the house, Frank thought.

But Bobbie wasn't back at the house.

The anxious couple drove around town that evening, honking and calling Bobbie's name until midnight. In the morning, Frank placed a newspaper ad. He was desperate—they'd have to continue their trip soon. They'd promised to visit more family in other towns.

"He'll probably show up the minute you leave," their relatives assured them. "We'll keep him until you come back through."

"Sure," Frank said. But inside he was worried. *Where was Bobbie?*

Nearly a month later, when Frank and Elizabeth returned to Wolcott, there was still no sign of Bobbie.

"Maybe he's all right," Elizabeth said tearfully. "Maybe someone adopted him."

Miserable, the Braziers headed home without their beloved pet. How would they tell their girls that Bobbie was lost or . . . worse? Could he be dead?

But Bobbie wasn't dead, although in the weeks and months that followed, he would face great danger. And he hadn't been adopted, though several families would try to make him their pet. And he certainly wasn't lost.

As it turns out, Bobbie knew exactly where to go. He had decided to walk back home to Oregon.

And there was no stopping Bobbie.

Bobbie walked nearly three thousand miles that fall and winter, crossing fast rivers and windy mountain passes. He walked through sunshine, rain, and snow.

He chased rabbits and other critters, but for food this time, not for fun. He stopped at farmhouses along the way, weary and thirsty, but he never stayed long.

On February 15, 1924, exactly six months after Bobbie was lost in Indiana, Nova and a friend were strolling in downtown Silverton when they noticed an old, mangy dog limping ahead of them.

There was something familiar about that dog. Something about his tail . . . *Could it be?*

Then Bobbie spotted Nova and raced at her. She dropped to her knees and he licked her face, making small, happy cries that said, "I can't believe it's you! I found my people!"

Nova followed as Bobbie rushed into the restaurant like a whirlwind. After a short, joyful hello for Elizabeth and Leona, Bobbie streaked upstairs to find Frank, who was sleeping after his night shift.

Bobbie leaped onto the bed, paws on Frank's shoulders, whining, crying, and covering his face with kisses. *Am I dreaming?* Frank thought. *It's impossible!* The dog's feet were raw and bleeding, his nails worn down to nubs. He was so skinny and dirty, his fur so badly matted, Frank hardly recognized him. But there was the scar from the horse hoof, and the one from the tractor.

It was a miracle!

Bobbie gratefully drank some water, then lay next to Frank and slept for hours. Later, Frank fed him a thick sirloin steak and a pint of cream. Bobbie rolled onto his back and held up his wounded pads, as Frank tenderly wiped on medicine.

For days, Bobbie slept and ate, and ate and slept, as he healed.

Bobbie's unbelievable story quickly spread across Silverton, then Oregon, then all across America in newspapers. Letters arrived from strangers. "We sounded the horn, and the dog ran up and jumped right into the car as if it was his own," one said. Another wrote, "He seemed to know where he was going."

Here and there, Bobbie had accepted a meal or a night's stay. At one house, he'd searched every room before eating and moving on. Some had wanted to adopt him, but he'd chewed through a rope or slipped out of a new collar.

"Listen to this," Frank said, reading to his wife. "'He was always looking for someone and always in a hurry.'" Frank reached out to pet Bobbie, who panted and offered a dog smile.

"And as we all know," Elizabeth said, "there's no stopping Bobbie!"

Bobbie curled up at their feet. He was home for good.

BOBBIE, 1921–1927

. . . the big Scotch collie dog belonging to Mr. and Mrs. G. F. Brazier, proprietors of the REO Lunch Restaurant in this city, surprised his owners one day this week when he showed up at their place of business after an absence of about six months.

—Silverton Appeal, February 23, 1924

Bobbie posed for publicity photos with Frank.
(Drake Studios/Vades Crockett Collection)

Bobbie's remarkable journey thrilled readers around the country, who wanted to know more about "The Wonder Dog." The Oregon Humane Society in Portland investigated and confirmed that he had traveled about 2,800 miles on foot. They presented Bobbie with a silver medal and keys to the city. Letters and presents poured in daily. Frank wrote about him in *Animal Pals*, a book of dog stories, and Bobbie starred in a silent movie. Bobbie's feat even appeared in *Ripley's Believe It or Not!* Bobbie got so famous that at one weeklong appearance, more than 100,000 people showed up to pet him

In April 1925, Bobbie became a parent with another collie named Tippy. She gave birth to *sixteen puppies*—all boys—and Bobbie made headlines again.

When Bobbie died two years later, hundreds attended his funeral, and Portland Mayor George L. Baker gave the eulogy. Afterward Rin Tin Tin, the dog star of twenty-seven Hollywood movies, arrived with a wreath.

In 1932, Silverton hosted its first Pet Parade to honor Bobbie, with his son Pal leading the way. Every summer since then, the town has celebrated with a parade and a Bobbie Look-Alike Contest.

Bobbie's Castle, his red-and-white doghouse, stands over his burial place at the Oregon Humane Society's animal cemetery. A statue and a seventy-foot mural in Silverton pay tribute to their famous dog.

The Braziers' granddaughter, Valena Crockett, visited "Bobbie's Castle," where the famous dog is buried.
(Ron and Chris Crockett Collection)

For Frank and Elizabeth's granddaughters, Valena Garver Crockett and Vades Dickerson Crockett, who dedicated themselves to keeping Bobbie's story alive for future generations. And to Ron and Chris Crockett and Dana and Donna Crockett, who shared their family legacy: a true story of ultimate devotion. —T. B.

For my lovely and patient wife, Karina.—C. P.

Text © 2016 by Tricia Brown
Illustrations © 2016 by Cary Porter

LSI2021

This paperback edition ISBN: 9781513277387

Library of Congress Cataloging-in-Publication Data

Names: Brown, Tricia. | Porter, Cary, illustrator.
Title: Bobbie the Wonder Dog : a true story / Tricia Brown ;
illustrated by Cary Porter.
Description: Portland, Oregon : WestWinds Press, [2016] | Summary: Bobbie the
Wonder Dog was a scotch collie mix who was lost on a family trip from
Oregon to Indiana and walked all the way home, nearly 3000 miles and six
months to the day he was lost, to the people he loved.
Identifiers: LCCN 2015034598 | ISBN 9781943328369 (hardcover) ISBN 9781943328376 (e-book)
Subjects: | CYAC: Collie—Fiction. | Dogs—Fiction. | Human-animal relationships—Fiction.
Classification: LCC PZ7.B8185 Bo 2016 | DDC [E]—dc23 LC
record available at http://lccn.loc.gov/2015034598

Editor: Michelle McCann
Designer: Vicki Knapton

Published by West Margin Press®

WEST
MARGIN
PRESS

WestMarginPress.com

Proudly distributed by Ingram Publisher Services.